METAMORPHOSIS

BOLD POEMS

APAR SINGH

Copyright © Apar Singh
All Rights Reserved.

This collection of poems is dedicated to the energy that I feel. This energy has liberated me, and given new wings to my imagination.

It's the energy due to which art exists in this world, and every artist craves for. Like my previous ones, this work too is dedicated to the same heavenly energy.

Contents

Contents

Foreword

Preface

All human actions have one or more of these seven causes: *chance, nature, compulsions, habit, reason,* **passion, desire** - Aristotle. Poems are like kisses. It's better to act **in the moment**, than to wait forever. We lose steam, we forget, and we move on. Well do we really, ever?

There's an adage that says - You can have anything you want, if you want it **badly enough.** How much is bad enough? I bet it's something to explore, when it's worth it. Quest for each unique want, leads one to a unique journey, resulting in a unique **morph**. We all have two lives, and the second starts when we realise we only have one!

There's no self in love and to find our real skin, we need free self from the **society's dreck** that's piled on us over the years. The world we find ourselves in, is replete of blather. So let the journey to morph begin. As they say some wrong trains take us to the right destination. Hope you board yours!

Prologue

Had I been your man,
Won't miss one night.
Never leave you alone,
Keep you in arms tight.
Had I been your man,
Would give sweet pain.
Love your entire span,
Keep busy narrow lane.
Had I been your man,
Morn-night peck & kiss.
Cheek by jowl, no clam,
Love thee, eternal bliss.
Had I been your man,
Swarm up to make hay.
Spread honey and jam,
Silk-rout-e via Milky way.
Had I been your man,
Eat, sleep, mow, repeat.
Nip peaks, ruin tunnel,
Bit by bit, layers peel.

Desire

When is it too late to feel, to desire? I say, never.

Desires are bred in open, and feeling hearts. A pulsating heart, a rushing mind, a crushing hunger, an unquenchable thirst, all compels for survival. Nothing is more real, more important and more essential than a desire. The vehicles of clairvoyance, desires are need, want and love.

1. C-C-C

Want to muss you up,
In a state of disarray.
Inside, let us blow up,
Fornication 'underway.
Wish being inside you,
Never be outstanding.
See in eyes, pluck you,
A boring, never ending.
My reeling desires to cup,
Tonight, passions screw.
Lift your slender legs up,
Push really hard through.
Can swallow you whole,
Suck both melons apiece.
Touch and lick your hole,
Making go weak at knees.
Yearning to rubble thee,
Melting lavas, meet sea.
Make you beg and plea,
Divine sounds of C-C-C.

2. Cling

I must not cling to you,
But miss you all times.
Try hard not to pursue,
Her divine light shines.
I will keep my distance,
Even when going crazy.
Get closer to desistance,
To hold you going fugazi.
I shall not unbridle you,
Whilst I go intemperate.
Recalcitrantly turn blue.
Never been so obdurate.
I should not think of you,
Barring days and nights.
Can I disrobe to rob you?
Picture lingerie, in tights.
I cannot see your distress,
Still, text you impromptu.
Words might not express,
What my desires are onto.

3. Boring

Will she mind, if bore her?
Can't stop self from asking.
Do it every day, assure her.
Her eyes leave me gasping.
Inviting is her fine waist,
I stare at deep sexy navel.
Right now, I want to taste,
Tear blouse & sari unravel.
Want to bite the rosy lips,
Her killer waist-ass ratio.
Throat her down till ribs.
She kneels down at patio.
Wish to press her bosoms,
Feel those pointed nipples.
Her lovely cooze blossoms,
Touch it & feels the ripples.
Mount her face wide open,
Overflow it with my spout.
Shotgun hers, until frozen,
She grabs it and I go all out.
She bunts her hands down,
Is used to getting her way.
To tickle, wrestle till dawn,

Hope she makes me stay.

4. Bed

I lay down in empty bed,
Replete of wild thoughts.
Dim light & shut my eyes,
Wish met her in aughts.
I lay down in unfilled bed,
What she'd be up to now?
Wish she's here to cuddle,
Snuggle & make her thaw.
As I lay in my vacant bed,
Who's untying her locks?
Wobbles, shiver, vacillate,
Find self-tangled, in knots.
I lay down in my bare bed,
Buss and whisper at night.
Pulse, desires past control,
Pecking dreams, feels right.
As I lay in my barren bed,
Does he drive you askew?
My wild desires roam free,
Wishing to canoodle you.

5. Dirty

Yawns and arches back,
Spreads open, legs wide.
She's longed for too long,
Lucky one will be inside.
Lunge her, clunge tight,
Giving her deep strokes.
Deflower her just right,
Touching all sweet spots.
I can feel her heartbeat,
How do I think straight?
So high, her frames heat.
Over me lays her weight.
We are all things nooky,
Rock hard, popping jelly.
Wrap her round finicky,
Fizz and cream her belly.
In this whole wide world,
None arouses me like her.
She plays it dirty and flirt.
None douses fire like her.

6. Good Life

When I am going all in,
Why you push me back?
As I am on the way out,
You again pull me back.
Let the dust settle down,
Before, touch her eyelid.
You're so wet right here,
My fingers' slip on, skid.
When you move away,
I pull you back like bad.
With each passing day,
Know what I never had.
Such tensions simmer,
We could even explode.
Often excusing myself,
Going insane with load.
I wished for a good life,
Fleetingly coming close.
In you losing my strife,
Never say never, adios!

7. Juicy

Her kohl rimmed eyes,
Tempting ruby red lips.
Wonder if she'll grip it,
Rubbing it on her tips.
Her nubile fizzog flair,
Run finger in her hair.
Smooch sultry tongue,
Biting her sensual ear.
Kills me by slinky smile,
Without fail every time.
Devouring slender neck,
Moving shoulder to spine.
Her slim fragile arms,
And long sleek thighs.
Shall grasp them tight,
Pinch her to new highs.
Her juicy petite bosoms,
Madly want to discover.
Tight butt in high heels,
Pluck them and uncover.

8. Kiss

As I feel her fingertips,
I long to pull those lips.
Untie hair, loosen clips,
Bite thighs and rub hips.
As her breath trembles,
Blood gush to my heart.
See her pointed nipples,
Her top wish to rip apart.
As I wrench her wrists,
Fell her body vibrating.
Each second she melts,
Fell her body pulsating.
As her knee's stumbles,
Push her back to a wall.
Now that she crumbles,
Ready to give me her all.
As her long neck caress,
Move my hands-on arm.
Unzip, unlock & undress,
She's frozen, as sea calm.
As her beauty she bares,
Shying of intimate parts.
Run fingers in her hairs.

Hasty love-making starts.
As we go down on other,
Bodies flare up like fires.
Enticing yawn and moans,
Feeling her unmet desire.
As make her hold it inside,
Feel passions in my veins.
Want her to feel high tide,
She too, can take the reins.
Deflowering, as she begs,
Pushing all of self-inside.
Tongue it down to dregs,
Heady roller coaster ride.
As she moans and pleas,
For me to start and stop.
It's a night of my dreams,
Until she blows me out.

9. Mole

There is a mole in hole,
Badly wish it was mine.
It brushes up her thighs,
Shivering up her spine.
There is a pole in dole,
Dreams of a cave always.
Never bends, stands tall,
Takes front & sideways.
There is a log in hands,
Needs her to be relaxed.
Rat the pussies all times,
Both waxed & unwaxed.
There is an irksome cock,
Hard as a mountain rock.
Slide it her mushy hands.
Give her a lifetime's shock.
Look at crazy sturdy dick,
Lately been acting a prick.
Runs thru her gams slick,
Give her life's biggest kick.

10. Screw

Once gazed at bare back,
How do I think straight?
In loving we're too slack,
To screw, endless we wait.
It's play-time, no refrain,
Tear apart sequin dress.
Feels goes down in drain,
Alone will make it a train.
Her tipsy eyes fuel me,
A handful & no quickie.
Slinky strides drill me,
Pull her erotic lingerie.
Slowly whisper in ears,
Why churn her to tears.
Hot and heavy in years,
Wild pleasure she nears.
She's a crazy situation,
Feels under a sedation.
Bored it deep and fatal,
Upended in fornication.

11. Shack

Need her down on me,
Throw her on bare back.
She can tear up my tees,
Tonight, let's get a shack.
To her I proffer myself,
Can make love, if no sex.
All loving that she lacks,
Know it's hard, just relax.
She can go wild and free,
Layers of her garms peel.
Hold redwood of my tree,
Keen, so raring vibes feel.
Who all came here before,
Know-not, what they had.
Wait for your yes to bore,
Care not a sofa or a bed?
We can both all night lay,
Can feel her heart pangs.
As a potter hardens clay,
Hold, suck, bite by fangs.

12. Thunder

Lost my precious sleep,
Coming out of slumber.
Incurious cuts me deep,
Strikes many a thunder.
In a ward, lay my focus,
Need her voice to heal.
Since became my locus,
In her eyes lies my zeal.
All time mind seeks her,
There is no peace in me.
Wish to make her spur,
Stuck here as times flee.
The more of her I obtain,
Try going further, yearn.
Desire makes me suffer,
Can't churn her, I burn.
She is my favorite book,
Body, soul wish to learn.
Ahead of her cover look,
Leaving no page to turn.

13. Tolerance

Yawns and arches back,
Spreads open, legs wide.
She's longed for too long,
Lucky one will be inside.
Lunge her, clunge tight,
Giving her deep strokes.
Deflower her just right,
Touching all sweet spots.
I can feel her heartbeat,
How do I think straight?
So high, her frames heat.
Over me lays her weight.
We are all things nooky,
Rock hard, popping jelly.
Wrap her round finicky,
Fizz and cream her belly.
In this whole wide world,
None arouses me like her.
She plays it dirty and flirt.
None douses fire like her.

Passion

Is you passion strong enough to melt them? Only time will tell.

Desire needs steadfast passion to make impossible, possible! Passions rule emotion, or emotions rule passion? It is the master of desire - taking over us, bending way of life to help find self. Passions are founts of youth that unleashes possibilities.

14. Clout

Lately up and about,
Awed by what betide.
Big men with clout,
Try lay by her side.
Many came and went,
She had a good time.
They lived in her tent,
She never gave a dime.
They all wanted to give,
For one thing in return.
Ahead of her conceive,
All her desires I discern.
Can't help but show off,
How none got inside her.
Being loved only to scoff,
Is she now a disbeliever?
She stays on other side,
Is rational and practical.
Imprisoned in her strife.
Hope she turn irrational.

15. Drug

Once you've tasted her,
Ain't a drug to move on.
Longed, long to kiss her,
Turning into black swan.
She loves me or teases,
Spares minutes in days.
I accept bits and pieces,
Under someone she lays.
I can either sink or swim,
May re-surface in a piece.
Hope ties to her to whim,
She is dicey and caprice.
She is the pool of energy,
Can dip in day and night.
Pulls me close like gravity,
Can I persevere her might?
We two need to go further,
I'll not talk anymore shop.
I shall ruffle her feathers,
Desires push me non-stop.

16. Ecstasy

Never had love or a life,
But I was self-sufficient.
Crave her in bed, a vice,
None ever so important.
Her voice is of essence,
In her selfies, penchant.
Find hard to rein myself,
How to unleash torrent?
Never did I pawn myself,
There's no worthy buyer.
For her display on a shelf,
Stares with her oft barter.
Can't touch self anymore,
On a word, proffer thuds.
I will come flying to you,
Via red eyes, early birds.
In extremis, I'm hell bent,
Ecstasy depends on her.
Morn-flag raises my tent,
Muse pulling her knicker.

17. Forsaken

Jabbed to a reeling pain,
Wonder a boon or bane.
Feelings oft hurt insane,
Reality, she veils again.
Fervid are highs & lows,
Desires grow too arcane.
She abruptly withdraws,
Beaching, now and then.
Killed by her back racks,
I find no fun to abstain.
Lately suffering setbacks,
Forsaken, time and again.
Turn dippy and unstable,
Being silly, beyond reason.
She acts cagey and brutal,
Wrecked, kallos indecision.
My Aphrodite and Athena,
Rending in her evanesce.
Lose energy and stamina,
Inequitable is her absence.

18. Incubus

Days she goes on-off,
Its incubus to breathe.
Elixir flowing in veins,
Can she feel the heat?
Days she screens me,
Wish to end and leave.
Wonder what are we,
Why at nights I grieve?
Days we do not talk,
Burn and churn inside.
Shows in face & walk,
I'm not the type to hide.
Days she doesn't call,
Shows she cares not.
Texts back a day later,
Her priority, says a lot.
My ask was some time,
Even in bits and pieces.
All I wanted was a smile,
She does as she pleases.

19. Jealousy

Kept awake last night,
This mornin, she yawned.
Wish arms were mine,
In there folded, moaned.
Tonight I try to sleep,
Will she bed him again?
For she'll be his keep,
Jealousy's drubbing pain.
Badly want to fill her in,
In more ways than one.
Although she needs a lot,
Sure, can give her some.
Today my sleep surrenders,
Devour me hell-hounds.
Beneath him she murmurs,
My envy is outa bounds.
She is picky and gourmet,
Craves a long *kaala-khatta*.
Champagne, she will spray,
I turn green-eyed monster :

20. Limbo

Want to tell my dimbo,
Stuck in her deep limbo.
It's a bitter-sweet place,
Mine one and only chase.
Wishing cute-tea stayed,
We could have both laid.
Missing scent every day,
Closer, even when away.
Reticence making crazy,
Turning sweaty & heavy.
Where shall I even start?
Miss pulses of my heart.
Looking forward to hear,
She's outa reach forever.
Mind's going to explode,
Bit by bit I seem to erode.
The craving is impossible,
Doesn't that feel terrible?
Can't lift a finger to write,
I've got nowhere to hide.

21. Pedestal

Turned needy & whiny,
Unsure of crossing line.
She became very slimy,
Pushed me back in time.
Keep calm and carry on,
Dealing with last strife.
I have loved, moved on,
Several times in my life.
She would not kiss me,
Like me, can't be bound.
Never said she loved me,
A day will come around.
If can reach my destiny,
Know-not without her.
So, ask her out restively.
Get passed over, forever.
She's above any pedestal,
Never, turns blind on me.
One among the celestial,
No way, turns deaf to me.

22. Mistakes

Can't sleep well of late,
Some beautiful mistakes!
Never sober, I turn rake,
This spell never breaks.
Each day going crazier,
Some alluring mistakes!
I'll try to make it easier,
Not a woman who fakes.
For a touch often sway,
New appealing mistakes!
This time going to stay,
Till desire she partakes.
Passion unlikely to fade,
More heavenly mistakes!
Secrets as we often trade,
Not a man who forsakes.
Dived too deep this time,
Many winsome mistakes!
Can surface back in tyme?
Relieve me of all my aches.

23. Slurp!

Her body want to lotion,
I care not for any notion.
Feed her a magic potion,
Am full of deep emotion.
Will lap you up, slurp!
In my bedroom or lawn.
Rip apart those clothes,
And not stop until dawn.
I want to dig you down,
In bathroom or kitchen.
Throw splashes around,
Drink from belly button.
It shall only hurt a little,
Unless you want it more.
Fragile frame's so brittle,
There'll be marks galore.
Inside, I want to drown,
Making your heart throb.
Roll tongues up & down,
Work clutching my knob.

24. Silly

I keep acting silly,
She bears with me.
I talk like an idiot,
She lets me be me.
I try dippy things,
She takes a chance.
I left her high & dry,
She's up for romance.
I am always dunce,
She keeps faith in me.
I often jump the guns,
She never gets narky.
I end up being a dolt,
She ignores dim-wits.
I get needy, desperate,
She senses my nitwits.
I turn into an imbecile,
She puts up, is astute.
I get away being crude,
She isn't one to dispute.

25. Suitors

Far too many she has,
No count of her suitors.
None suits grand plans,
She cares not for lucre.
Each season adds some,
And some she drops off.
Wears color of love often,
Break to see it wear off.
She leaves them in lingo,
Shows clemency to none.
Though she's a nympho,
Gets nooky with just one.
Knows not, this crazy lad,
Has fallen head over heels.
He knows not what love is,
Day after day, layer peels.
Tries to make her merry,
He's taken one-way flight,
Urged to pop her cherry,
If lucky, could get it right.

26. Passion

A first and last rapture,
Love her head to heart.
An unmatched pleasure,
Discovery is, but an art.
Leaves heart in ripples,
When her eyeball darts.
Bring in her hair tipples,
Fantasy, touch her parts.
Let me lift your legs up,
Strikes me as torn apart.
Tightly grip, both hands,
When we end, we restart.
Mirrors me in both eyes,
When I look inside hers.
Bite from neck to thighs,
Pulsating on, as she spurs.
Sweet sound her anklets,
Dopey like heavy opioids.
Making her go breathless,
Luscious, succulent spots!

Metamorphosis

A friend, a philosopher, a guide with a heart of gold, a real person is no less than alchemist!

Passion and desire are unnecessary evil, blinding & binding heart. Ever heard of philosophers stone, then you must have wished for one. Who wouldn't like to turn ordinary into gold? It takes a gem, an inspiration, an energy to help us see and strive for our self-worth.

27. Attachment

I am afraid of attachment,
Having built border walls.
She too has upped fences,
Intruder, named *love* calls.
Emotions' tough at times,
Facing prior a tough luck.
Lovin' is hard sometimes,
Barely managed to chuck.
These feels' uncalled for,
Why trouble her and me?
Losing ones, we cared for,
Two of us turned rummy.
Years on, lost our chances,
Of desires, feels of bonding.
We both sucks at romances,
Neither is up for pretending.
Her excuse is need of space,
I kick myself for impatience.
She ends up playing too safe,
I'm tired of paying obeisance.

28. 1000 storms

What do I risk for you?
Everything I have on me.
My past, present & future,
I beg, I plead desperately.
Luck has burnt through,
Not having a clue of why.
Time in 1000 storms flew,
To live, I didn't even try.
What do I have to proffer?
Carrying a baggage on me!
Might look like a moocher,
Stuck self in waters muddy.
I need to borrow one light,
Ne'er behind excuses hide.
Will not let go sans a fight,
Only wish for you, subside.
I am replete with big risk,
Like a ticking time-bomb.
Rousing power of basilisk,
Eye to eye, enemy aplomb.

29. Bear

When I can't bear myself,
How could she bear me?
Years on touched herself,
Wish I was there for thee.
She needs a load of me,
My love can't be resisted.
Hard for her to brace me,
Heavily she is contested.
Oft worry for a divvy,
Unlike me, she writes not,
I take it all out in a diary,
Unlike her, I fight it not.
Each time we get closer,
Pulls are hard to restrain.
Feed each other's zeal,
She can, I cannot refrain.
Days we somehow get by,
The nights, inchmeal crawl.
Days, weeks & months fly,
Fancy her touch up, befall!

30. Cried

My eyes had dried up,
Tried, yet couldn't cry.
Neither did in sadness,
Nor in moments of joy.
A lit evening told her,
Have cried often since.
Careful what you ask,
She can grant any wish.
Cuts deep across heart,
Lie not, no word mince.
Lost oft in her thought,
Remember her, I wince.
Cherish her company.
Upending her absence,
Someday 'll accompany,
She can't be past tense.
There's no sign of her,
Unsure if I lose or gain,
She has no time for me,
What is love but a pain.

31. Disdain

I talked far too much,
Took away all mystery.
She never said much,
Hi-story, no chemistry.
I chased her so much,
It took away her chase.
Only to never recover,
Stuck in friends' phase.
I treated her too well,
Leading to her disdain.
Spurns at me then on,
What did I really gain?
I am a mane-less lion,
She never really cares.
Always longed for her,
Never got a lion's share.
Made many a mistakes,
Wishing we meet again.
Plans that never worked,
Glad that, we made them!

32. Fears

Living is much more,
Than delving in fears.
Better pass over rigor,
Been on hold for years.
Often calm her down,
Listen and feel griefs.
Always works a charm,
Like none she relieves.
Learn to blindly trust,
Take risks with other.
Allow cracks in crust,
Try believe in forever.
Feel my love and lust,
You are music to ears.
Infinite feels, can't rust,
Mortal body, end nears.
One another glass pour,
Play stare-game in loop.
Esse to give you a sore,
What's lost shall recoup.

33. Flawless

She likes to work hard,
Both, in and out of bed.
The world she's warred,
Only wish, could be had.
It's no drama, but a flair,
Can pass days in her hair.
Bed, sofa, futon or chair,
Only if, she'd let me near.
She is flawless at work,
Melting her youths out.
Ceaseless at every club,
Sweats, vim and abound.
Her beauty and lit mind,
How can one ever miss?
To a rare gem self-bind,
Only if, she'd let me kiss.
With grit face hardship,
Disposition rubs on me.
She opened feelings up,
Often, goes MIA on me.

34. Pain

My love has no boundary,
And it knows of no rules.
Bring to her face ecstasy,
Devastate her using tools.
In her is comfort and pain,
Soul shatter-mend in time.
Blow her like a hurricane,
Want to slay her in prime.
Sans her is loss & no gain,
Life turning too mundane.
Would walk away if could,
Her aura keeping me sane.
In days I wait for nights,
At nights can't sleep well.
For abidance love fights,
I'm bailing self out of hell.
She provokes me insane,
Invite to eternal pleasure.
Blood flow can't restrain,
Pains, none can measure.

35. Persuade

I can be your safety net,
If you ever wish for one.
You shall never repent,
Could be your only one.
Whenever you feel weak,
I will help you stay strong.
Our code shall not tweak,
Make arch back, last long.
I know you're a lioness,
And you too need a lion.
You, no one can possess,
Need a lover to rely on?
In growth and expansion,
Never shall stand in way.
Wish to help anyway I can,
In your team, want to play.
Work hard to build success,
Lazing around, I'm a failure.
I'll keep trying, nonetheless,
Persuade, and win you over.

36. Reminisce

Once there was light,
A darkness now rules.
Gone out of my sight,
A creaking door fuels.
She used to walk-in,
Brought energy along.
I reminisce stalking,
No synergy's around.
Nights I can sleep off,
How to get thru days.
It isn't gloomy winter,
No fun in sunny days.
Resolute; won't come,
To provenience spots.
But here I sit smoking,
With her in thoughts.
I won't get by like this,
To fire need be closer.
Want no useless roses,
Miss my dearest clover.

37. Sun

You're like a second sun,
I feel you from far away.
To light up worlds burn,
Orbit you night and day.
You confer every season,
As we move near and far.
Root of medley emotion,
Come too close and char.
Spin around you forever,
You are sustenance of life.
A lively lover to discover,
Every morning and night.
Without you I'm stopping,
Lose myself every second.
In darkest voids dropping,
Again, hitting a dead end.
The center of my universe,
Gravity pulls me back to you.
Post millions of revolutions,
You still don't need me, I do.

38. Metamorphosis

I was sleeping awake,
Day dreaming all time.
Untold her unfolds me,
Hope, stays by my side.
She lives life and loves,
Manifests what's worth.
Does what's to be done,
Moves sierra and earth.
A curious serendipity,
Knows no fear or pain.
Her upending fortuity,
Lucky me, reborn again.
Shall crack on pursuit,
Need her back in sight.
Trusting my gut, intuit,
I saw in eyes that night.
Her memories haunt,
I can't say that I'm lost.
Instead found purpose,
I was so far, one ghost.

HALTING

EXHAUSTED
EX-HOW-US-TED?
TOOBAD
MY-BED-YOUR-BED?
LIFE
TOO SHORT TO LIVE?
LOVE
TOO RARE TO GIVE?
DISTRACTION
D-IS-TRACTION?
FRUSTRATION
F-RUST-T-RATION?
RUMPY-PUMPY
N-EVER HAD DEAL?
PASSION
W-HOSE T-HERE TO FEEL?
MISTAKES
MIS-TAKES?
FALSE-HOPES
FAL-SE-HOPES?
THROWN
OUT OF A SPINNER?
HALTING
NOT NOW, NOT EVER!

www.ingramcontent.com/pod-product-compliance
Lightning Source LLC
Chambersburg PA
CBHW061443160726
47995CB00003B/1024